blue

blue

POEMS
ERIN WILSON

CIRCLING RIVERS
RICHMOND, VIRGINIA

CIRCLING RIVERS

PO Box 8291
Richmond, VA 23226 USA

Visit CirclingRivers.com to subscribe to news of our authors and books, including book giveaways. We never share or sell our list.

ISBN: 978-1-939530-25-7 (paper)

ISBN: 978-1-939530-26-4 (hardcover)

Library of Congress Control Number: 2022935099

Cover art:
Blue Heart, by Kathleen Loe
Collection of the author

Inside art:

Photos Hiraeth 1, Hiraeth 2, Liam Painting, by Erin Wilson

For Ana, my first born,
and for Liam,
also my first born

Out of the deep, my child, out of the deep,
From that great deep, before our world begins,
Whereon the Spirit of God moves as he will —
Out of the deep, my child, out of the deep,
From that true world within the world we see,
Whereof our world is but the bounding shore —
Out of the deep, Spirit, out of the deep,
With this ninth moon, that sends the hidden sun
Down yon dark sea, thou comest, darling boy...

— from "De Profundis," Alfred, Lord Tennyson

CONTENTS

zaffre

blue

lapis lazuli

[scribbling on the underside of an eyelid

after Sokurov's film, MOTHER AND SON

such intimacies are more glaring than human life
and are, rather, god-like (wounds)...
beautiful, too, in the way tears catch light...
(one would never say any of these things. one would sound
    ridiculous. but here, where no one is listening, truth can
    stand, shakily, on colt-like limbs, flanks dripping with
    water)
you would understand this, yes? be careful...
be careful. be careful. wade slowly in. as though into a river]

Lapis Lazuli

I touch dew
and I touch the perfect body.

I strike flint
and I touch the perfect body.

I touch wood, breathe it, burn it, smell it again
and I touch the perfect body.

I plunge my hands in biting river water
and I touch the perfect body.

I bang stone
and I touch the perfect body.

I cry my past in stony tears
and I touch the perfect body.

I wring my hair toward the future
and I touch the perfect body.

I lay my body upon the man's body
and I touch the perfect body.

We make the perfect body.

[a hurt of angels

For me, it's beyond doubt that if my demons were chased
away, my angels would also be a little, well, just a little bit
afraid.
— Rainer Maria Rilke

privilege with new made was I
beginning the in

me from glistening slid he
slid I, glistening

?angels the were where

?lamppost the beneath Jesus that was
dark was night the

begged I
in set pains birth the when

lost was I

(myself know didn't I)
myself, know didn't I]

Blue

There is a family story.

When my first husband and I were together,
we hiked a fairly arduous trail with the children,
young at the time.

At the top, our daughter,
believing she saw water in the distance,
ran toward the jutting precipice
and nearly jumped.

It was sky.

My ex caught her.

There is a second part to this family story. There was a second
    child running.

The father's arms were already full.

Five

i.

Delightfully, after you tug upon the curled white string
waiting for the prize to be set free from the hilltop
(that you perceive as a mountain),
leaf litter up to your knees,
you hold the tampon out before you
as though you might hypnotize me.
You are five pretending to be seventy,
"Now, just who might drink tea up here?"

Little misunderstood things like this are darling.
You are darling, whose cup runneth over with Oolong.

ii.

Only dark things move through the dark night, reproducing,
boosting one another, darkening darklings,
dark on top of dark. You hear the floorboards being
herded to the barn's stall out back. You hear dark
animals shuttling. Black milk shunts in ribbons
to be sucked up by dark creatures for sustenance.
You see hooves.

When a head tips back in ecstasy,
you're hurt by a blood-bed housing long white chompers.

iii.

Even though it is a cross between a community center
and a living room (albeit lacking a couch),
you are initially shaken with fear.
That is, until you walk up the aisle
and lay your hands upon the casket.

With your face tipped forward
death's gleam shines up from the *it* and upon you
as though lighting your chin from a buttercup.

How relieved you are, "It's not Grandma; only plastic!"

You rise onto your tippy-toes so that you might touch
the marbled chartreuse bowl that once held her.

iv.

You *like* to be scared.
Not really.
Well, you like to be scared on a schedule.

For hide and seek you stand in a closet,
tell me not to be afraid,
then jump out.
You like to hide me in the laundry basket
then wonder where I am.
One time I am upstairs in your bedroom.
You run downstairs to get an apple,
then when you come back I am standing,
in plain sight, but in a new location.

You cry and cry.
There are no words to console you.

v.

We lie on the couch, heart to heart.
You plump my breasts then use them for pillows.
Your weight begins to labor my breathing.

The soles of your feet graze my ankles.

"I'll always lie like this, Mommy."
"Yes," I chime, "we will always, always lie like this."

How to Love Without Violence

I will not straighten the toys or insist on the rules.
I will not mention what the world wants, nor will I think it.
I will not pick the crumbs from your shirt.

Child, look at me. How do I love you without violence?

Your hair is messy. I shall kiss it.

I shall write this poem about your messy hair:

> your messy hair
> tells me
> your essence is busy being

I will become so infected with this poem,
with your essence of being,
that I will forget to brush my hair.

We will keep birds in our hair, nests without cages.

> All day long, we will fly and sing!

Vowels in Treetops

i.

You're playing beneath the arbor
that trains the lilac branches overhead,

imagining you're discovering
dinosaur fossils,

brushing, with a dry paintbrush,
the sidewalk

that's cracked and crumbled
with weather and time.

"Come here," I urge you to unfurl
from over your bent legs

to find me watching and waiting for you
in the porch swing.

I want to tuck you, dirty little thing,
into my body, an ingot, and sing with you.

My mother's strongest praise
about my childhood was that,

although I was seen, I was seldom heard,
a generational bias.

This is one reason I am so intent
to be near you,

to inherit your griminess,

to celebrate together,

body to body,
sound in sound.

ii.

Sometimes: pine and pine.
Sometimes: pine and poplar.

I have walked a thousand miles
beneath the canopy, pining,

until I arrived at this understanding:
what was lost — was not me,

and what was found — was not here,
but rather — the meeting.

Today, wind.
I would like the world to have a word

for the sound emitted
between two trees grieving,

the place of in-betweenness,
between *family* and *keening*.

The wind arrives
at the edge of the woods.

I pause and wait
for the wind to work the tallest trees,

which in turn push their kin further onward,
a malleable wave.

When the wind comes forward,
and the two that support one another

make that sound [   ]...

[   ]... that sound again,

I know it and name it,
a *kinning*.

Tea and Dinosaurs

in memoriam Mrs. Gross, and for my son

"Can we go, Mom? Can we?"

I gauge the three faces, their intentions.

"She's gonna give us tea," the seraph-faced one says, surly.

My son hangs there, pure, with hope.

"Ya, go ahead," I say.

And as though my words are cocked and I have pulled the trigger,
they break from the patio door and round the fence, a rag of colts.

"Use your manners," I call to the bottoms of their flashing feet.
"And be grateful," rings through the air.

It is quiet here
for a very long time,
a deep and eerie silence.

They pour back into the house, autumn wasps, somewhat
stunned, wicking through the cracked door, unzipping their coats.
I half expect to discover their midriffs to be chunks of amber
flecked with the stupefied inclusions of ants or bits of flowers.
They are slow, thoughtful, somber. Before they are disrobed, one
looks up and spills, "She put milk in the tea!"

Another shakes his head, amazed, "And she talked and talked for
hours!"

"Ya, the whole time," notes the third.

My son comes close and asks, "Did you know she was born in this house? And she owned an ice cream shop in town? And that it's not even standing anymore?"

"Yes," I say, "neat, isn't it?"

He looks unsure, "She talked a lot but said the same things over and over."

"Yes," I say.

His friends shake off their shoes.

"She kept asking my name and who my parents were."

"Yes," I say.

"The tea was good," he offers.

"Yes," I agree, helping him out of his shoes. "It was a very special time."

He speaks as though to the glass in the sliding door, "I don't think she'll remember."

In the evening, my son and I watch a show on television about the extinction of the dinosaurs. He cries when I put him to bed. I ask him if it is because of asteroids and stuff. He says, "No, it's just that when I close my eyes, it comes behind them, as though it's real."

"What?" I ask. "What do you see?"

He answers, "Nothing—"

Anthropocene Lullaby

The child knew nothing
except that he wanted.

And that which he wanted
was far away.

And that which stood between him and his desire
hurt him.

He saw his hands were pink in the morning
and black at night.

[what are you
      darling boy?

   whatever you are

they will come for you

      no shield is tensile enough

they will come for you

      no tenderness is shield enough

they will come for you

      for heels, for chest, for hands,
         for heart, for mind

they will come for you

      be ready, be you,
         be blue]

Twenty-first Century Boys

He's in a tree.
Trying to climb a tree.
"It's hard," he cries.
He's slipping.
His father's getting mad
for lack of progress.
The tree is dying.
Everything below him is dying.
He is trying to climb a tree
and not trying to: *climb a tree.*
He is trying to do everything.

Everything wears a dash of ash and so is slippery.

Seven

Seven is a mystical number.
Mystical numbers overflow with themselves,
a bounty of being and vulnerability.

No mother wants to hurt the number seven.

This is the last winter your father and I will be together.
You and a friend are sitting in a snowbank out in the yard.
You told me you were going out to play your guitars.

You sit close together in your snowsuits,
holding your guitars up and shaking them.

Are you playing music or warding off birds or inviting them closer?

That night you will have me listen to your first performance.
You will sit on your bed with your seven-year-old legs dangling
and have me listen (not able to see you) from the hall.

The next day, with your sister's encouragement,
you'll invite me to listen to you play in the living room.
You will warn me first, eye to eye, "Mom, I'm really good."

This is how the number 7 is shaped.

Nine

L: "Mom, if you won tickets to Wintersleep, would you go
   and see them?"

Me: "Certainly!"

L: "What if they were playing in France?"

Me: "Oh, I'd love to go to France."

L: "Really?"

Me: "Yes! Why not?"

L: "Well, I would go, too. But only to see the mimes."

also nine

All year, a winter of grief.

I find him on the floor and stroke his hair.

"I don't know why, Mom."

[a prayer whispered from the future

we're both childlike
playing on the rocky shore
of the river,

boy-child
and mother-child.

confused
by wild joy,

I spot the bear
and alert you,

"run closer!"

confused
by danger,

"no, no, away!"

confused again,
always confused, "closer!"

the bear does
his little dance of desire
on the opposite shore.]

River Water

September 27, 2013, a Friday:

Four times today
he laughs
from the pure chasm of his throat,
head back
forgetwhoyouare laugh.
Forget everything.

A pure white bar
extends
between here and joy.

It's Late

The curtain between our rooms is open.
I have fallen asleep with my broken glasses on,

holding *Anna Karenina*, heavy in so many ways,
its pages rifled open but eased back into the blankets

like a sleeping infant, my own hands yet creased
as though around a bottle. You have forgotten

why you've come in and so instead just say, "Mom,
remember when your moccasins were too big for my feet?"

Playfully you demonstrate you can't even
squish the width of your toes inside them.

We both seem amazed that this was the truth
and now the truth has changed.

You leave. The curtain falls.
I take my glasses off.

Remind myself to wrap your birthday presents in the morning.

Birdsong

I pull the blanket
from his shoulder
and off his broad feet
and touch the
nearly-forbidden skin,
newly exposed,
as I have been doing
every morning
since his birth.

Outside a bird empties
a little of its sugar
out of a sac
from the branches
of our basswood.

"Do you hear it," I ask.
"Yes," he nods.

He nudges away from me,
nosing back into his sheets,
closing once again in on the zero
of his personal sleep.

"Well, as you drive into the city,
don't forget it."

Elegy for the Easiness of an Early Evening

Mother and child walk down the country gravel road
in the early evening's empty hours of   bird furls

doing nothing but kicking up   dust   and notes
which are the silent spaces   and swirls   around the rising dirt

    the music of muteness and touching

they're bumping happily into one another
fumbling love in their hands   in their empty clodlike hands

stroking penumbras of golden light   lifting   rising   caressing
to the smote of shoulders   errant hairs   and the private
    folds of clothing

and there they are walking down that road
going nowhere but through that place together

holding up the last of the day's cambered light with their
dumb ripe hearts   in love with skin that but runs together

there on that dusty road   so clearly   so painfully
never again   you and one of your own small children.

Eerily Dark with Forward Illumination

A band of storm clouds
moves along to the east,

a celeste yarn in warp,
a navy blue in weft.

Closer to me,
our little bank

of under-developed sunflowers
is suddenly illuminated.

Can't see the sun though,
so where does the light come from?

Watching them bob and pulse,
it feels as if

my cheeks are lit too,
a secondary light-soused decoration.

A blue jay, a blue-tipped white arrow,
pierces the street's stillness.

I snap a shot
and text it to my son,

captioning it: *eerily dark
with forward illumination.*

Then the whole vignette gets tamped.
Rain patters its Morse code over earth.

Wind sweeps inside our house and rattles
the metal blinds that bank our windows.

blue

The Young Somnambulist Speaks Softly Now

The color blue
has forgotten its hands.

Attached to its stumps—
nothing.

    Therefore, in its heart—
    nothing.

    Therefore, in its mind—
    nothing.

    Therefore, out of its eyes—
    nothing.

    And where the color blue's eyes should be—
    nothing.

Now measure your sadness.

Try to tell me your grief,
that cuts you at your wrists,
is more.

Just try.

Orphaned Rabbits

When I speak with my son at his dad's, in Ohio,
his voice has changed. He sounds unfamiliar to me, a man.

But he sends me selfies
of such a tender boy.

Manlet, as he calls himself.

He rescues a bunny from his dad's backyard,
the mother having been killed in the front yard
by his black cat, Mystery —

funny world of balancing.

He keeps it for a few short days, in his room,
in a blue Rubbermaid tote, with bedding, food and water.

He sends me static photo after static photo
of just his hand gently passing over the bunny,
so much smaller than his own hand.

(Triggered body memory — I know his fingers like water.)

    One can perceive, even from this distance, a deep
    trembling.

He shares a video of the downy little thing, disoriented.

I convince him to turn it over to wildlife handlers in the
    morning.

    How sick I feel. How powerless. For this. For everything.

In the morning he wakes to discover it drowned in its water
    dish.

    It seems to me that one must widen (or narrow?)
    to adopt an animal's sensibility, in order to survive what,
    in its strictest sense, *seems* like a godless world.

Over and over I think,

This is what there is.
                    There is this.
Or there is nothing.

Blue Heart

Masculine or feminine,
I make no claim.

You took him to the shooting range.

You knew what I thought.
You knew what I'd say.

You took him to the shooting range.

You put the heavy weapon in the small child's hands.
You hit him on the back for a job well done.

You took him to the shooting range.

Every morning before school,
every evening as homework.

You took him to the shooting range.

You, the dad, the man,
you put the heavy weapon in the small child's hands.

You took him to the shooting range.

All night, while he dreamt in bed,
you took him to the shooting range.

Whatever "it" was, whatever "it" is,
you tried to kill "it" out of him.

You took him to the shooting range.

The Moose Calf

Not to be born is the best for man;
The second-best is a formal order
— W. H. Auden

Then, is it enough to say, we see this?
That reality holds the mirror still,
and still holds the mirror, always?

This: not a deer, as my son thinks at first glance.
I see the shape of its head as we are passing —
hurtling too hurried to stop,
too tightly packed among the cars and trucks
throwing up a slurry of slush and muck on Highway 17,
between the temporarily erected meridians
directing traffic through late-season construction —

see and recognize the elongated face of a young bull moose,
who knew no better than to test the ice too early,
its bulbous head budding horns, stubbornly swaying
its burdensome weight, attempting to ballast its body,
half-submerged in lampblack winter water,
between two thin bridges of ice, working
its ponderousness against the current and cold.

We are past before we can be sure it takes foothold.

Could Auden have known? Will time, circumstance?
Does language, might nature —
that *moose* is borrowed from the Algonquian languages,
moosu, meaning *he strips off*?

There are other sights along the road I know from previous
    journeys:

a beaver lodge humping the placidity of a purely black pond,
cattails lashed roadside to bob,
an abandoned gas station
I have longed for years to shoot with film, snow-covered
and framed by tangled berm and heavy heads of see-sawing
    sumac,

but it's the bull calf's struggle that tests, falls through, rises,
    penetrates, sinks, resurfaces,
and then reruns again and again in my mind,
as I usher my son on to the hospital with thoughts, again, of
    suicide.

Specifically, and Scattered Fragments
I Hate in My Notebook

i.

I Think "Teeth," "Tools," "Clatter"

He undresses.

He gave himself
a new tattoo,

a sad monkey.

He lies back.

He counts his ribs.

He takes
every
last
piercing
off

and places them
in the bowl of his belly.

ii.

A Scenario

A little boy
follows
his mother
into
the examination room,
responding to her, "follow me,"

with, "why why why..."

Moments later,
the emergency doors open
to his sharp cry,
"Why?
Why?
Why?"

      iii.

One Way Out

We wait for the doctor.

Not able
to help my son,
I turn to an elderly patient,
a stranger,
and rub his back.

I buy Henry some soup
and a coffee.
He does not like the cookie
I buy him.

Henry winks
at all the young girls.

      iv.

Specifically

An important difference
I cling to,
as though to a ledge.

When asked,
he does not say,
"by jumping,"

but,
    "falling."

Some Kids

in Crisis

For hours two kids in the hall push a big red ball
back and forth. One girl says to me, *I like your hair.*
As I'm walking by, a mousy child in their room mutters,
And I like yogurt! They raise their cup like a wine glass, cheers.
Another kid, a little guy, instantly everybody's kid brother,
rushes from room to room, manically occupying
other people's spaces. The adults vie, "We don't do this,"
as they try to keep pace with him, but remain
precisely two steps behind. He locks the door.
Oh, oh. Someone pushes the button. "Security to the
fourth tower!" No one but me seems to mind the alarm.
They laugh or carry on with their books
or cards or lying there, blank-faced, doing nothing.
(It is, after all, isn't it, all quite alarming.)
Each patient has turned over their shoelaces.
Every parent searches for clues.

There's an us.
There's a them.

My son writes in the window, *I'm a vegetarian
and just ate a burger. Things must be dire.*

White Sheets

One night.
One night is the head with an eye-door.
One night like every other,
you fold the eye-door
and lay it in the dresser,
blessed quiet sweater.
One night you close the drawer,
climb into bed.
One night every chicken in the coop
sleeps, little moons tucked into puddles.
Feathers are layered.
Feathers are laminous.
Feathers are countable and foreseen,
compose a complacent fan.
No fowl will disturb you.
One night is one night is every other.
One night is sanctified.
One night is moth-eaten, platitudinous.
One night is portal, safe passage of time.
One night is sealed, is a sealing,
the ceiling is white, a vestigial christening gown.

 One night the eye-door is ripped open.
 One night and always that sound — torn tape, wrecked
   adhesive.
 One night and always the filling of a vacuum.

One night he comes to you,
his eye-door having torn
every living fowl to pieces.
Feathers are severed fingers.
Bloody, he crawls into your bed.

Body, he crawls into your bed.
Moon-slick with bloody feathers,
he crawls into your bed.
A thousand reflected moons, bleeding.
His heart is a wounded bird.
Proof. You feel it.
It is beside you.
It is tragic under cover.
It is trying to get back to the eye-door.
Around your naked legs it writhes, beheaded.
Around his neck, headless, a cowl,
your quiet sweater rived to ribbons.
One night lanugo blue and crematory red fix the heavens.
One night an apocalypse in the orange trees.
One night a screaming from empty spaces.
One night every eye-door! Time is stymied.
One night accesses every other.
There will always be an injured bird
struggling for resurrection
in your little bed.

The Shearing

This is as close as we've been in a long time, frontal bone,
   temporal line, slopes of parietals.

He's not speaking to me.

I'm speaking with him with the warmth of my supplicating
   fingers.

Between us it's happened in increments, the cutting off of
   his long hair. Underneath everything, I find his father's
   hairline.

(Get the fuck up off the carpet or you won't amount to anything!)

The clippers drone. They have a protective covering over the
   blades, so there won't be bleeding.

I think, *There is only blood.*

As his last locks fall, he becomes, once again in my hands,
   something somewhat fetal.

Which is how I found him last night.

In the dark, I only dared to touch his peripheral,
   hold his bones in sackcloth.

Now, in stark daylight, I pass a blade over him.

zaffre

Clair de Lune

> the still moonlight, sad and beautiful
> — Paul Verlaine

A heavy eye-lidded morning,
god pushing his thumbs down again,
keeping the light out
but for the penumbra
surrounding the dull orb.

And if there is no god,
a weather system?

Last night, sad
because your son was sad
and sitting alone
closer to the cold moon
in his attic room,
you Googled, an act
of self preservation,
songs like / or as good as /
Beethoven's "Moonlight Sonata."

There was a full moon.

You sat downstairs
on the couch,
a moderately light stone
delicately anchored
and hurting.
So much pain amongst the stones.

And Beethoven. Gone. Debussy.
Schumann. Liszt. Bach—

/baχ/

Also, Glenn Gould would come.
And go.
Only notes
and his father's chair
linger.

And this today: your daughter,
your happier child,
went out into the cold.
Before, looked for
but didn't find
her white earmuffs
that now rest
on your mother's old mahogany table
that survives
here with you
beneath the frosted window,
two snowball things
on a wiry branch
that do not melt.

Atoms for Adams

Because of when I was born
my mind seems at home thinking
atoms are about the smallest things.
Atoms, only a placeholder
anyway. Meanwhile, through
the outer corridors of science
and semantics, *quarks*
have been whizzing along.
Listen: once Empedocles thought
earth, air, fire and water
were everything, and Thales
thought it was water alone.
Does it really matter?
Pussy willow, I say
into the oncoming of spring.
Dark matter, Mrs. Sharma
swelters, taking Mr. Sharma
erotically into her many arms.
Something enters something.
When I lie down to bed
and feel the weight of the
thousand sorrows, yours,
not mine, I scoop a luminous
cradle of sparkling seems-like-
nothings into my palms.
I put my face to them as though
looking upon a moonlit pond,
and I breathe, Please, dear
little building blocks of civilization
that floss continuously through walls
and conversations, do your work
and transgress the worried skein

of his mind, carry aloft
the heat and moistness from my
mouth, the same mouth that
once kissed his rumpled brow.
Carry these light-harboring
black seeds in a child-drawn cloud,
the smallest luminous energies
that will—*live*.

So Much Depends Upon

Usually I have to wake him, and he is often cold and angry,
not a morning person.

This morning he is already standing in the kitchen
when I awake.

"I don't know, man.
It's been a rough morning."

I gauge his expression.
Am I really this ready to be afraid?

Yes, I am.

Behind him by his feet
is dirt from a plant.

Also, to his side,
spilt milk.

He's nearly naked in his bare feet and underwear,
hand-sewn shirt open over his thin and perfect body.

He says, "Everything went wrong this morning.
I spilled the coffee creamer.
Then the coffee spoon stuck to the saucer.
The saucer fell.
Knocked over this plant."

He motions with his foot.

I see the plant now, a small cactus,

lying on its side beneath the counter.

It could be enough to break anyone,
a nettlesome green, black earth, spilt milk...

And yet something at the corners of his mouth tugs.

Slowly, I reach out my hand.
He responds to this and reaches out his hand.

We shake hands.

I say, "Well, I wanna thank you.
It's been a good run."

"Ya," he agrees, "a good run.
Now I'm gonna kill myself."

He stands amidst the chaos, scratches, and then asks,
"Hey, do we have any William Carlos Williams?"

Defense Against the Black Arts

i.

These are the facts.

Something came from what we perceive to be nothing.
Nothing is nil, cool. Something is warm, here.
The bridge between buckles.

Sometimes this is also true.

Something is terrifying as hell.
Something is a bolus-of-bats with fangs
being flung at us up through our medullae oblongatae.

What's throwing it?

We look down, see our own dumb hands,
headless roosters

ii.

This is also true, though, I think, maybe, sometimes.

There is no such thing as nothing.

iii.

Vermilion, viridian.
They get to know us at the Buck or Two.
Sap green, burnt sienna.
The aisles are a refreshment of things, of order.
Notebooks, sketchbooks, reams of paper, brushes.
Phthalocyanine green, phthalocyanine blue.
Carmine, crimson, cadmium yellow.

Canvases, canvases, canvases.
Lampblack. Mars Black. Iridescent Graphite.
(Only sometimes, only sometimes.)

Let us return safely to the ochres.

[vade mecum for the fledgling

something like: cello, violin, piano
something of: solace, self-worth, purpose
    sonata
    a sense of togetherness

if you could carry with you…
if you could believe…
if you could see reflected…
if you could hear…
if you could play…
if you could create…

the body's made of veils and openness
the wrists are green
they want to be caressed
they want to be planted in
they long for new growth
they dream of dreaming

if you are going to decorate yourself…
if you are going to make your best chance…
wear rain upon your nakedness out into the sunshine
wear nakedness over your burlap tunic of hope]

The Flower's Bargain

It must be strange being on the cusp of becoming an adult,
for it is strange to be an adult on the cusp of becoming old.

On the one hand, her face is opened innocently, like how
the convolutions of a rose give light back to its rosebush.

And on the other hand, it is dark and clever, working
machinations in involutions and folds.

"So, like, if he dies" (watching
my face), "like" (pause) "in a car accident" (notes

the holding of breath between us),
"you have to promise me not to kill yourself."

Uniforms

The boy with the wild curly hair, silver rings and home-modified
clothes, goes to work with the burly men for his first job.

He tells me three of them ride together in the truck today
and because he is the smallest, he sits in the center.

The foreman drives. The other lad is a strapping fellow
from a nearby farm. The men talk about

their johnsons. My son confides the talk is terribly uncomfortable.
"Mine is like a button in a fur coat," the foreman explains,

mostly in jest. The guy to the right gets into it pretty good.
I wonder if the foreman is silently laughing.

My son says nothing, laughs at nothing.
Just rides along, deciding what it is to be a man.

Crime

It is not your father's fault.

It is not my fault, my inability to socialize, my leaving your
    dad, my strangeness with the world.

It is not the fault of the body that your father made.

It is not the fault of the body that I made.

It is not the fault of the body that we made for you together.

It is not the fact that polar bears are starving.

It is not the fault of Februaries, your birth month. (*February*
    sounds with *cruel*.)

It is not the fault of the political right.

It's not Spiderman's fault. (Duh, the Tobey Maguire version.)

It is not *___'s fault for teasing you about your earring.

It is not the fault of the piercing. That skin grew over when
    you took it out.

It's not *___'s fault for lauding you for having "like, the whole
    world of knives" as a collection, or being the best at drop-
    kicking a ball.

It's not Grandma's or Uncle Tom's or mine or Dad's fault, for
    giving you various knives.

It's not origami's fault. (Remember that first how-to book
    James gave you.)

It's not Dad's fault for not letting you get a tattoo. It's not
    my fault for letting you. (But a fault line lies between the
    two.)

It is not the fault of the needle you sink into your skin. Nor
    the ink's fault. Nor the train's on your chest, the bone's on
    your shin, the ghost's on your arm, the sad monkey's on
    your ankle. The John Lurie character your girlfriend gave
    you is new and so certainly is not at fault.

It is not the fault of art books or Jim Jarmusch.

It is not poetry's fault, although as much as it has given (me),
    in terms of time, it has taken.

It's not even weed's fault. (But maybe alcohol's, a bit.)

It is not the fault of the zipper tag you choked on when you were
two. The ambulance attendants had nothing to do with it,
nor the nurses, nor the doctor. The X-ray machine was only
doing its job.

It's not the fault of your dual citizenship.

It's not Christmas trees' fault, real or synthetic.

It's not casts' fault (you've had two), nor carp's fault (that big ugly
fish you were good at catching), nor dog's fault (Bones'), nor
cat's fault (Fox's, Meow Meow's, Louie's, Socks's, Maggie's,
Roger's).

It's not the fault of the cobalt blue poison bottle catching light in
your bedroom window.

Your eyes are blue. Your hair is curly. The blue sky is empty/open.

[via negativa

perhaps I should have apologized for my inadequacies
and left it at that

I was only ever a constellation of freckles,
a parcel of horse muscle

what I wanted for you
was only what I wanted for myself

there is no solving for X

a loaf of bread + a loaf of bread
equaled your small body

a loaf of bread + a fire
equaled a bird in a wood stove

between all things: a shovel + an apple,
a needle + a brick]

Boy Impastoed

I don't realize it
until it is almost over.
(Is it almost over?)
How you were being
buried in paint.

That time,
that terribly violent
time. You gasped up at me
out of the night canvas,
at the stoplight,
not far from the McDonald's.
(See all of the lights,
the red tail-light warnings,
the yellow humps of piss-stain,
in the terribly
pedestrian universe.)

I was ratcheted
from my silence,
in an instant
nearly stillborn,
a white gaudiness,
upon the beat
that might have been
your annihilation.
(Literally, you were listening
to "The End" by The Doors.)

> Then months of pain
> and bouts of prescriptions.

Now that I hear your voice
return,
I sense the daubing
that was smothering your body,
    sometimes black,
    sometimes white,
is allowing you to return,
become realized once more.

You metamorphose
    visible,
your trickling voice
    a draft
once again
    filling
your precisely
    cambered chamber,
beloved blue-hued bottle.

A Study of a Boy with Two Eggs

My hands are cold
as I sit at our
wooden kitchen table
early morning,
reading about Ruskin.
I have been
preoccupied lately
with his study
of a Danish bowl,
painted circa 1871,
becoming
periodically healed
when I've cut through
the funk
of any given moment,
to truly *see* it.
His *study* of it,
the dainty blue
detailing
the lustrous
white porcelain,
such an elevation
I'm excited, dizzied.
I want it in my hands!
Although
it's not cracked,
a kintsugi power
exudes from it.

My son is downstairs
with me, early for him,
frying up some eggs

in an old black
cast iron frying pan
handed down to us
by my mother.
He has bare feet
on the cold floor.
I can't imagine
choosing such a thing.
I hear the oil.
I steal a glance at him
choosing one egg,
and then another.
I hear the cracks.
He works
the metal spatula
against the pan.
The smell
of cooking egg
fills every living space.
Such simplicity
and yet,
this act is monumental.
Ruskin would say,
"It is only by labor
that thought
can be made healthy,
and only by thought
that labor
can be made happy."

A few minutes
after my son departs

with his plate,
I rise
and press my hands,
through the residue of eggs,
to the dark pan,
for now
a warm place.

Dear Issa,

Your poem about dew
is the world
And yet...

The summer mornings are becoming cooler. I am driving
my son to work, and then I will sit amongst the goldenrod
and bullfrogs, waiting for my work to begin. The farm fields
we're passing sparkle with dew, a consequence of the cooling
weather. Now spiderwebs, substantial, stand out, simply
because of moisture. I begin to understand you, Issa. This is
very likely my last summer with my son.

Threshold

A wish from a mother to her two children
upon their departure

I wanted dust motes. You want dust motes. Dust motes for
you.

Bach's cello will eventually become essential.

Candles, matches, wax, linen, turmeric, salt, pepper.

Who anticipates the bitter bent wire of red wine?

Surprising (mis)communications by bedpost.

Particular shoes on particular floor mats.

Schedules
and the grating of schedules
and the fleeting retreats of schedules that ejaculate
like choruses of scruffy crows
wheeling amidst glutinous angels.

The majestic ball and the complacent socket
and the complicated synchronicity of moods.

The failed pie, delicious.

The cut and confiscated pine tree.

The pumpkin's contagious orange.

Something unexpectedly dead and stuck to floorboards.

The tactility of a notebook cover
and the aromatic discovery of —what? —what?

Strobing sunlight, the novellas of windows.

Thrift store linguistics.

The humorous awakened
and the humorous stupefied and snoring.

Toast. Heartache.

Quotes from Ginsberg and the Gospels.

Mahogany, oak, maple, dark walnut.

The pressing desire for togetherness
and freedom.

Everything.

Jacquard

It displeases me that he smokes,
so he smokes only mugwort.

He is working an O'Keeffe print
from an old *Life* magazine.

The flower now smells of ash.

What he cuts bears a cauterization
of his, and his alone, hands.

He frames the flower, *Black Iris, 1926*,
and a little bit of the accompanying text.

Hangs it.

Then we carry in the couch.

There are two sides to the cushions.

He could place them beige side-up
but instinctively prefers the sprawling floral print.

We sit beside one another and consider
O'Keeffe's work:

    it's a fire wearing an iron chastity belt,

    a snapshot of coral reef with undulating seaweed,

    how my labia still carry the christening
    of his cranium.

"Nobody sees a flower—really —
it is too small—we haven't time..."

He lights one of his shabby
hand-rolled cigarettes. Inhales.

Burning inherits the edges.

The Sound of Thunder

A heavy rain
slows cars
as they wind home.

Drivers turn their wipers on high.

I wander
from window to window,
opening, closing.

Your rooms...the whole upstairs,
I thought they were the best rooms...

But I can't love the rain,
heavy on the shingles.

I can't love the rain,
abolishing the roads.

I can't love the rain,
harrowing this willow.

I can't love the rain.

And I can't love these rooms.

When the rain started,
I thought I might.

But I can't remake the past.

You were not happy here.

The windows are empty.
The rain is empty.
I am empty.

Milk

i.

Grime: foul matter that mars the purity or cleanliness of
    something;

crud, filth, gunk, muck, smut,
scrum, sewage, swill, slime, sludge,
dross, dust, grot,
colly, crock, soot,
dinginess, dirtiness, filthiness, foulness,
befoul, begrime, besmirch,
gaum,
confuse, disarray, draggle,
contaminate, defile, pollute, taint...

It's not *dirt.* I don't mind dirt. Although it's dirt too:
plant dirt on the baseboards, refuse in the heater vents,
paint on the floors, spilled and agglomerated
I-don't-know-whats everywhere, banana peel stickers
stuck in windows, apple cores embedded in bed sheets,
tape on tacks on bus schedules on posters on walls.
(I had to peel a notebook from a notebook, loosening a
    splotch of
some not-meant-to-be-adhesive adhesive, two notebooks
I gave you two short months ago, never opened, but already
defaced, disheveled, undignified, sullied, to begin this poem.)
It's the untidiness of things no calm mind might have
    brought havoc to:
antiques in ashes, jackknives gaumed closed, empty paint cans,
Matchbox cars with broken chassis, half-syruped Cokes, dead
    cell
phones, bent albums, rusted hand saws, slack-stringed guitars.

ii.

Your new room, ground floor apartment
of a century-old Arts & Crafts house,
is a milky white duvet cover
and eight painted white window mullions,
vignettes staged here and there: a purposefully
unfinished portrait of you sketched by your girlfriend,
stacked collectors' tins, a vintage cobalt blue bottle
(empty, marked *Poison*),
an old book with a leather skin, a succulent,
and dahlias (is it?) in a vase on your dresser
bobbing their cheery, colored heads.

iii.

Grime, near antonyms:

decontaminate, purge, purify,
straighten up, mother.

My fingernails are filled with grime.
I feel the weight of it, the chaotic volume.
I don't know how many glugs of water from this pitcher
I'll need to pour, how many rolls of paper towel to reach
the wood on the desk you've left behind.

iv.

As the story goes, my mother (Grandma) can't stand
the taste of milk. It's not the milk itself
but milk as signifier. It's wrecked by association.
She says, "I can't look at a glass of the beautiful stuff
without smelling cow shit." And so her bones —

I don't know — what, grow brittle?

I don't know how this vignette fits in, but here you go,
a muntin; go figure.

v.

Somehow I couldn't do this for you, my familiar,
your space, your room, so alien to me now,
so unfamiliar. I feel like an astronaut
rooting through moon rubble:
rogue socks, dismantled artworks
(clippings of Francesca Woodman and Francis
Bacon), dead wasps, empty Doritos bags.

I tried last fall when you were gone, admitted, *in crisis.*

But when you came home, you shut the door
and through mental magnetism,
your bedroom   your bedlam.

vi.

Milk —
as an infant you just wouldn't take mine.

Perhaps I didn't try hard enough.

vii.

Why today, I wonder. I don't truly know.
This morning there was a pitcher of gladiolas
from a Mennonite farm in our kitchen, nine stems,
one pink, one purple, four orange, three red.

A strong urge to know
each magnificent unraveling spire in pure light
came into me, an engorgement.

I carried them up here.

I hadn't realized the physical dissonance of your mess
could dwarf the rightness of light through this,
our house's best window.

As I wrench things to garbage bags,
wipe down walls and windows and lamps and
even the candle stick I work into an also-wiped-down
wine bottle, Tranströmer's words spark and linger in my mind,
the tail-end of a sparkling bright comet,
"Vi tjuvmjölkade kosmos och överlevde"
("We secretly milked the cosmos and survived"),
Swedish lessons that I left off
last fall
        with your fall.

Blessings Derived from a Military Obstacle Course

for Liam and Basil

Writers on parkour trace its origins to the physical
education and training methods developed beginning
in the years before World War I by Georges Hébert and
known as "la méthode naturelle." The regimen involved
... the use of obstacle courses called "parcours du
combattant."
— from Encyclopedia Britannica

The final goal...is to make strong beings.
— Georges Hébert

The tiny bunny
that now lives with him in his bedroom,
that sometimes shits in the sawdust, upon the bed, in the
    carpet, on the linoleum,
that enjoys throwing his ball with a bell
and takes full advantage of his parkour circuit (shoe box to
    shoe box to Liam's mattress to floor again)
to finally rest in his second little bed (a cigar box) beneath a
    chair,
knows nothing of the rabbit
that died years ago.

A Prayer for the Wayward

The young man lowers his hand, gently
redirecting Basil, his bunny,
guiding him back toward being
(what we deem from our human stance as)
not-naughty, all without words,
no, Basil, don't eat cords;
don't pee on things, Basil;
don't hump mother's purse.

I think of this and other things
(like how I overstep and *advise*
regarding the thermostat or washing dishes,
or how I unsuccessfully, time and again,
try to be funny), guiding my mind
between awareness and self-criticism,
my mind an ever wily little thing
coated in nervousness,
jack-knifed by a need for love.

I could never be a monk, I think.
But the young man, with his dangling hand,
manages being,
and the brown bunny arrives in this world
already dressed in monk's robes.

Hearth

My God, a whole moment of happiness! Is that too little
for the whole of a man's life?
— Fyodor Dostoevsky

You two are walking up the sidewalk,
an old man walking beside you, chatting;
because you're so young and healthy and open
he wants to shelter near you;
who wouldn't want to shelter near you,
you, so much taller than her,
your thin cotton summer shirt open
over your thin white undershirt,
wearing your girlfriend's floppy hat
that moves around your face like sunflower petals
or shines out from you, a corona of your happiness together,
her beside you, kerneling toward you,
so much smaller than you, protected by you
and a seed or gleaming pit of interest and potential;
happy, you are both so happy and so beautiful,
I see from the car, watching you together
this unguarded moment, moving along the sidewalk,
smiling with the old man who is a fire to you
too, a reflective kind of fire or an inglenook
to your earnest flames, young and warm and open,
a crucible, a burning.

The Dream

after "The Dream," by Marc Chagall, and "Liam, Unfinished,"
by C. R. W.

*...there was less of it in terms of mass, there was greater
spiritual density.*
— Louise Glück

More than any candid shot,
or story,
or memory (except perhaps
the half-forgotten ones),
the unfinished
painting of him
draws my attention.

What is there
is only the suggestion of
a few bones,
knit together
by a color swatch
of skin possibilities,
maybe, at best,
five-eighths of his face
portrayed.

I fly toward him, my arms out,
soaring with the density of a Chagall character
through indigo space.

If I can just keep moving
toward him, drawn by the pull
of where he isn't,
I will reach him.

[poem whispered to the loved one

if I could secret you
in my skin,

if I could show you
how I fly with ravens,

if I could convince you
the thousand years
we're tied to stone
is but a moment,

if I could make it clear
all shackles dissolve
with the proximity of just one
thimble-sized angel,

I'd trace the tattoo you wear
beneath your skin
that assures, you too
(perhaps most of all),
are chosen.]

A Little Warmth

February has cracked
one of its bright cold days
over my window.

Now the snow banks
are a theatre stage
and I must decide
about my costume.

The winter birds
have their say,
percolating
their clear liquid music
invisibly
against the glass.

It is silent,

then Arvo Pärt's
Cantus in Memoriam
Benjamin Britten,

then silent again.

I drive the two and a half hours
through the cold
to fry eggs for you.

Blue, Redux

Are you kidding me,
we got you through those
tough years,
and now there's going to be
a pandemic?
Are you kidding me,
we got you through
that severe depression,
and now this?
Are you kidding me,
all those nights
with the stink of weed,
and me looking
the other way,
all those nights
with the dead eyes,
and me searching
for a pulse,
all those nights
with you in an undershirt,
and me with the car keys ready?
Are you kidding me,
we got through those nights,
and now this?

There's a life-size
blue elephant
painted on the wall,
and I'm not fucking looking.

And I Was Sore Afraid

I dreamt you hacked off your hair again.
I knew what that meant.

What was left was still intensely curly though,
heavenly so.

You gestured to your right side and asked,

"Did you notice, shaved into the side of my head,
an angel?"

There was one broad wing, as though the angel were moving off,
or drawing near.

Gold

after Leon Wyczółkowski's painting, "Spring in Gościeradz"

i.

We speak of art, as we make our trip.
We speak against erasure.

You thumb through a tattered volume of lesser-known
    painters
as we pass one wide, flat farm field, after another.
Even when only gently, the snow blows,
wiping out the uniqueness of each farmstead,
overcoming even the bulk of hibernating machinery,
John Deere, Massey Ferguson, Kubota.

At times we have to guess where the road is.

You were born in this town and we've not been back since.
How right it feels to make this trip as a birthday gift,
after all your grief and turmoil.

ii.

History at the antique shop glows, the oil-rich wood of the
    egg crates,
the matrix of cardboard inserts still intact—and this holds
    something off, doesn't it?—
as do the red-handled rolling pins, the sturdy glass of the Fire
    King bowls,
the green and gold to-be-sewn-on badges with emblems of
    moose and beavers,
the time-softened postcards, their precise script, official
    stamps,
the baker's hutches, enamelware teapots, rusted cow bells as

heavy as human heads.
A primitive blue painted cabinet is jam-packed with rolled up
      carpets, four rugs
spilling out onto the floor. We stop, altered by awe, tracing
      their elaborate patterns.

We spend hours threading the three levels of furniture,
      ephemera, bric-a-brac,
the smell of homemade macaroni soup stitching us to our
      own narratives,
as the proprietress walks a bowl to her husband (who suffers
      from dementia)
waiting for her at an oval oak gateleg drop-leaf table, in a
      private, cordoned-off area.

I watch you thoughtfully touch things, being touched by
      things, being mended.

Days after I drop you off at home, the first lock-down begins.
Now, still in winter, wondering when we might be together
      again,
I write to you, revisiting Wyczółkowski's "Spring in
      Gościeradz."

*That pear tree outside his window burns, a golden fire. The flowers
in the vase are doused in flame, too, as are the curtains, the chair's
upholstery, the open book resting in the window.*

*The tapestry burns its brightest where it's most abraded, and gold
leaf, a debris of stars, shines, shaken, an invitation, all over the
wood-worn floor.*

Remember upstairs in that antique shop, those intricate old rugs we loved, that had been rolled, then lobbed, a shelf's worth of dark spirals?

They're still there, awaiting the light.

Pastoral

In black boiled wool, we are walking
the farmlands together in winter.
I prattle on about Andrew Wyeth.
The winter grasses. Well, you know winter grasses...

Maybe it is like those old gold sheriff badges.
Something of me was hammered into a gold star,
and that gold star was hammered into you.

Everywhere we look: white expanses,
bunches of pale yellow bromegrass and fescue,
electric lines breaking into kestrels, ravens, crows,
flying stars that spread into the fine striations of feathers,

    that land deftly like rivets driven into barn boards.

We both dream of living in a barn someday.
I am being nostalgic. You are dreaming of the future.
Golden thread, holding fields together, stitches friably
    through snow.

Contemplation, Ending with an Angel

after a photo of James, Betsy, and Andrew Wyeth standing
before the painting "Faraway"

I close the book that I had been tilting toward the lamp
to light the way the paint lies on the page
and lay the book to rest atop my lap's blanket.
It's the book about the Wyeths, three generations.

I take my wire frame glasses off, rub my eyes.

Then I pass the left arm of my glasses around the left side of
    my face
and then hook the right arm over my right ear again.
The maneuvering of the metal makes that sound
that metal glasses do, in their being adjusted.

I open the laptop and strain to see. I am tired.

I begin to tap this letter out to you:

"I forgot to tell you, today while I was walking,
I came across crows making all sorts of odd vocalizations.
They sounded just like two gorillas conversing.
(It can be a strange world, but crows can do this.)
Then, like that other day on our walk, suddenly—
the sharp-cut sound of flapping wings!"

Mortar

Do I keep it secret enough,
that I want to infiltrate their bodies,
and stay like the happiness of fat
along their hastening-away-from-me bones?

Galette—a large pie crust
topped with fresh Swiss chard
(tossed with thyme and olive oil),
diced onion, red pepper, ricotta and feta,
the edges of the crust free-form,
but partially folded over to restrict
size, shape, vegetable body,
brushed with egg yolk,
baked 'til golden brown.

I made the dough at home,
my mixer's dough arm
ploughing the lard and flour
together, making this brick,
that I froze, and then thawed
in the back window of my car
on my way to visit them.

I get the rolling pin from my purse
and work/push/press
its familiar work-harmonics into air.
Do they notice, I wonder,
these amber-inebriated, horse-hooved bodies
that, on their best days, wear their twenties
as lightly as flannels?

Saving Lives

How many times in a life is a single body born?

———

His thin arms are still quaking when I arrive,
just moments after the paramedics have left,

as though the whole of his body
has just squeezed once more through the birth canal.

It is painful for me to note this aftermath,
but I am always eager for knowledge of him.

As he speaks, his hair harnesses and casts light,
falling in its unkempt tatters and curves.

While other kids around here his age are busy posting memes,
getting laid, driving cars,

he works honest jobs, caregives stray cats and rabbits,
restores guitars,

sits in the early morning light on his front porch
as strangers bustle by with bouquets of flowers.

———

(20 minutes before)

"Don't be afraid," he whispers to the man who has fallen to
    the sidewalk
clutching his chest.

He cradles the stranger's head, strokes his hair,
neither sure if this is the last hour.

———

He is busy saving lives. More than the stranger's.
More than his own.

The Job of Motherhood

i.

Giving away all the furniture
perfects the living room.

Hunger
perfects the taste of almonds.

Mondays perfect Sundays.
Wednesdays perfect Sundays even more.

Herons perfect
faithlessness.

Grasshoppers
perfect cities.

Bears, and the sure bulk of bears,
perfect Wall Street and Academia and portfolios.

Indifference can be perfected
by petrichor.

Moving away from the entanglement of our limbs
makes our love a bell of ice and diamond.

ii.

In order to perfect things
we must move away from them.

It can't be true I ever resented either of you for waking me
and taking up the space of me.

I see you down the aisle in the grocery store
as a stranger would,

your adult limbs a bafflement of beauty—

and each time I would choose you.

If you want a happy ending, that depends,
of course, on where you stop
your story.
— Orson Welles

Zaffre

My grief is blue
Your grief is blue
Our grief is not the same color...

[touching the body perfect

let's come back to the beginning, shall we?
you hear? not go back, but come back.
in the way a flower sutures itself through memory
back into its sails of scent and mystery of color.
or the way a ball rediscovers its stitches sealed tightly
akin with the lifelines in the palm of the pitcher.
if we travel far enough out into the darkness—

we circle the earth.
we come home. that's what this all is.
one great homecoming. where we trade names,
addresses, faces. where, after every fracture,
we make family. where despite. despite. despite
whatever the clamor/tumult/terror is. despite.
there is this. now. here. between us.]

Acknowledgments

Poem | Original publication

Anthropocene Lullaby | *The American Journal of Poetry* (Motive issue)

Birdsong, Five, It's Late, Jacquard | *At Home with Disquiet: Poems* (Circling Rivers, 2019)

Blue, Orphaned Rabbits, The Shearing | CBC Poetry Prize, longlist

Vowels in Treetops | *Channel Magazine*

Threshold | *Crab Creek Review*

[scribbling on the underside of an eyelid] | *CV2*

Milk | *Hole in the Head Review*

Atoms for Adams, Five, Jacquard, White Sheets | *isacoustic*

A Little Warmth | *Juniper*

Pastoral | *The Meadow*

Hearth | *Poetry Scotland*

Gold | *Symposeum*

The Moose Calf | *takahē*

Zaffre | *Temz Review*

Boy Impastoed, Clair de Lune, Defense Against the Black Arts | *Triggerfish Critical Review*

[poem whispered to the loved one] | *The Wild Word*

So Much Depends Upon | *You Are a Flower Growing off the Side of a Cliff*

Quotes, in order of appearance

Alfred Tennyson. *Poems of Tennyson.* Boston: Houghton Mifflin Company, 1958.

Rainer Maria Rilke. *And, Nonetheless: Selected Prose and Poetry 1990–2009*, by Philippe Jaccottet. Translated by John Taylor. New York: Chelsea Editions, 2011.

W.H. Auden. "Death's Echo." *Collected Shorter Poems, 1927–1957.* New York: Random House, 1967.

Paul Verlaine. "Clair de Lune." *Fêtes Galantes.* 1902.

John Ruskin. *The Stones of Venice.* London: Smith, Elder & Co., 1851.

Georgia O'Keefe. *An American Place* (exhibition catalogue). 1944.

Tomas Tranströmer. "Fire Scribbles (Eldklotter)." Translated by Patty Crane. *Bright Scythe.* Louisville, KY: Sarabande Books, 2015.

Parkour entry, from *Encyclopedia Brittanica.*

Fyodor Dostoevsky. "White Nights." Translated by Constance Garnett. *White Nights, and Other Stories.* New York: Macmillan, 1918.

Louise Glück. "Night School." *Three Penny Review.* Winter 2020.

Orson Welles. *The Big Brass Ring: An Original Screenplay.* Santa Teresa Press, 1987.

CPSIA information can be obtained
at www.ICGtesting.com
Printed in the USA
LVHW042005200922
728862LV00005B/282